Wild Animals

RATTLESNAKES

BY LIBBY WILSON

WWW.APEXEDITIONS.COM

Copyright © 2023 by Apex Editions, Mendota Heights, MN 55120. All rights reserved. No part of this book may be reproduced or utilized in any form or by any means without written permission from the publisher.

Apex is distributed by North Star Editions:
sales@northstareditions.com | 888-417-0195

Produced for Apex by Red Line Editorial.

Photographs ©: Shutterstock Images, cover, 1, 4–5, 6, 8–9, 14–15, 16–17, 18, 22–23, 24, 27; iStockphoto, 7, 10–11, 12, 13, 20, 25, 29; Paul Williams/Science Source, 21

Library of Congress Control Number: 2022910614

ISBN
978-1-63738-443-5 (hardcover)
978-1-63738-470-1 (paperback)
978-1-63738-521-0 (ebook pdf)
978-1-63738-497-8 (hosted ebook)

Printed in the United States of America
Mankato, MN
012023

NOTE TO PARENTS AND EDUCATORS

Apex books are designed to build literacy skills in striving readers. Exciting, high-interest content attracts and holds readers' attention. The text is carefully leveled to allow students to achieve success quickly. Additional features, such as bolded glossary words for difficult terms, help build comprehension.

TABLE OF CONTENTS

CHAPTER 1
WARNING RATTLE 4

CHAPTER 2
SKILLED SNAKES 10

CHAPTER 3
LIFE IN THE WILD 16

CHAPTER 4
DINNER TIME 22

COMPREHENSION QUESTIONS • 28
GLOSSARY • 30
TO LEARN MORE • 31
ABOUT THE AUTHOR • 31
INDEX • 32

CHAPTER 1

WARNING RATTLE

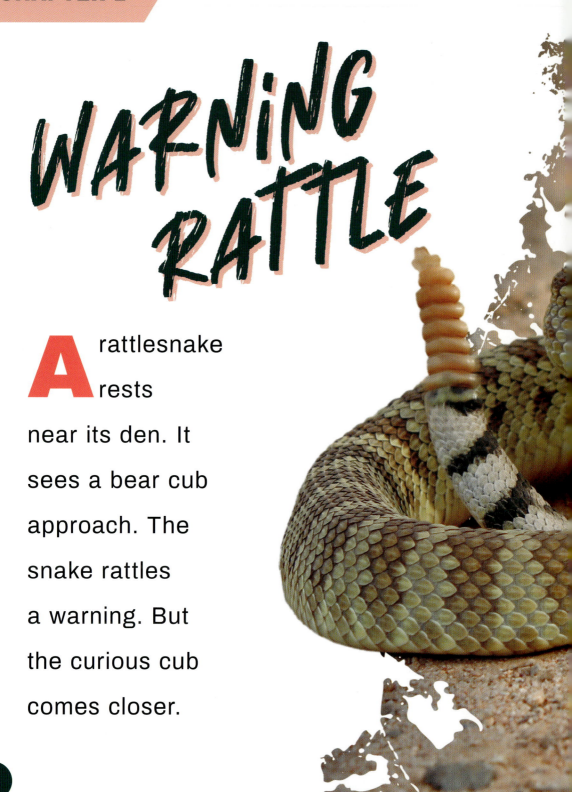

A rattlesnake rests near its den. It sees a bear cub approach. The snake rattles a warning. But the curious cub comes closer.

Rattlesnakes shake their tails to make rattling sounds.

A rattlesnake's fangs can be up to 6 inches (15 cm) long.

The snake gets ready to attack. It moves its body into a coil. It hisses wildly and shows its fangs. It backs towards its den.

FAST FACT
Some rattlesnakes spray stinky liquid to defend themselves.

Rattlesnakes curl up their bodies before they bite.

The cub flees. The snake relaxes. It didn't have to use its **venom**. It can use its deadly bite to hunt later.

Rattlesnakes will bite if they need to. But they prefer to run away or hide.

DANGEROUS FANGS

Rattlesnake fangs are hollow. Venom flows through them. The fangs lie flat most of the time. When a snake bites, its fangs pop up. They send venom into its prey.

CHAPTER 2

SKILLED SNAKES

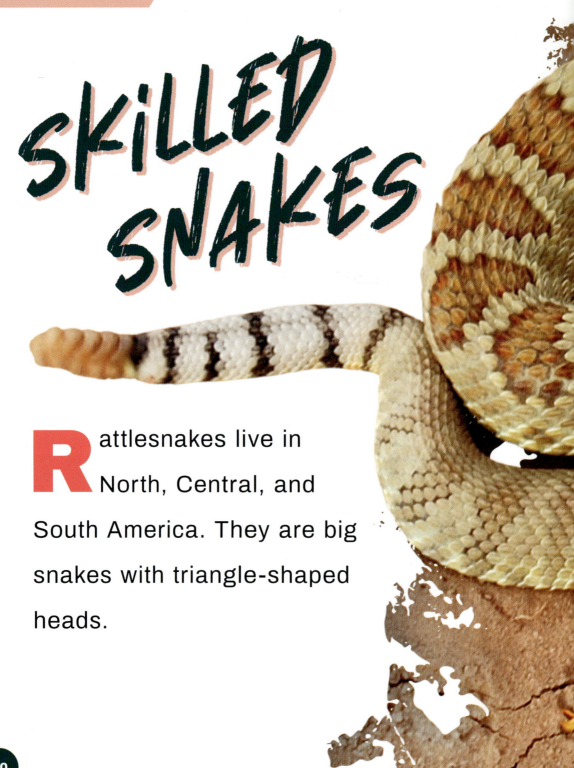

Rattlesnakes live in North, Central, and South America. They are big snakes with triangle-shaped heads.

A rattlesnake's scales often have stripes or diamond-shaped patterns.

Western diamondback rattlesnakes blend in with rocks and sand.

There are more than 30 kinds of rattlesnakes. Their scales have different colors and patterns. That helps them blend in with their **habitats**.

SIDEWINDERS

Sidewinders are rattlesnakes that live in deserts in North America. Their name comes from how they move. Their bodies skim sideways over the sand. Only small sections touch the ground at a time.

Sidewinders make curved trails in the sand.

Each rattlesnake's tail ends in a rattle. This body part is made of rings of hard material. When the snake shakes its tail, the rings knock together. They make a loud sound.

FAST FACT

A snake's rattle is made of the same hard material as a person's fingernails.

A snake's rattle gets bigger each time the snake sheds its skin.

CHAPTER 3

LIFE IN THE WILD

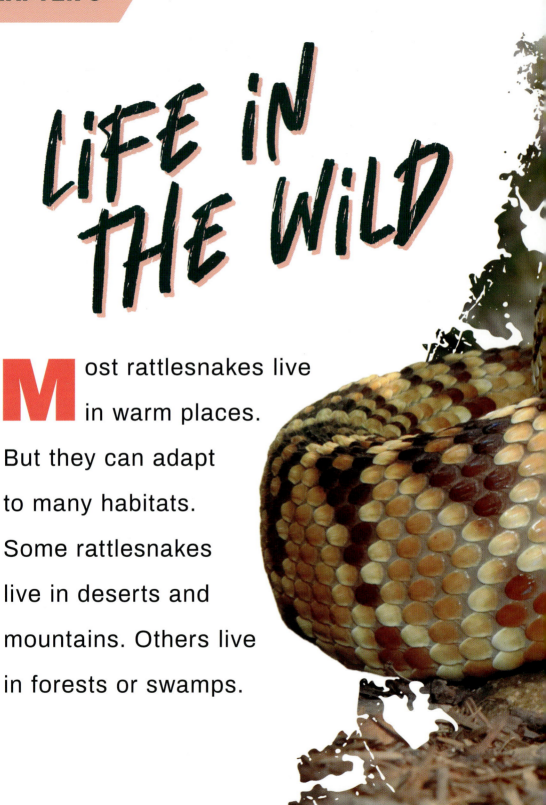

Most rattlesnakes live in warm places. But they can adapt to many habitats. Some rattlesnakes live in deserts and mountains. Others live in forests or swamps.

Northern black-tailed rattlesnakes sometimes live in forests.

Like most reptiles, rattlesnakes are **cold-blooded**. They bask in the sun to stay warm. They cool down by hiding under rocks.

WINTER SLEEP

Some rattlesnakes live in snowy mountains. They may **hibernate** together. They rest in dens during cold months. One den can have hundreds of snakes.

◀ Rattlesnakes come out from their dens in spring.

Male snakes may fight each other to mate with a female.

FAST FACT

Rattlesnakes live about 15 to 20 years in the wild.

Newborn snakes stay with their mothers for less than a day.

Rattlesnakes spend most of their time alone. But they come together for mating season. Female rattlesnakes give birth to live babies. The young snakes live on their own almost right away.

CHAPTER 4

Dinner Time

Rattlesnakes often rest during the day. They hunt at night. They eat **rodents** and other small animals.

Rattlesnakes often catch and eat rats and mice.

Rattlesnakes use their tongues to pick up smells in the air.

Rattlesnakes can use their sense of smell to hunt. They wait for prey to come close. Then they strike. The venom in their fangs kills the prey.

FEELING HEAT

Rattlesnakes can sense their prey's body heat. That's because they are pit vipers. These types of snakes have small holes on their faces. These pits sense heat from nearby animals.

A pit viper has small holes between its eyes and nostrils.

Rattlesnakes eat their prey whole. Their jaws have stretchy joints. The joints let the snakes open their mouths very wide. After eating, rattlesnakes rest and **digest** their food.

FAST FACT

A rattlesnake only needs to eat once every two weeks.

A rattlesnake's skin can stretch when it swallows large prey.

COMPREHENSION QUESTIONS

Write your answers on a separate piece of paper.

1. Write a few sentences describing the main ideas of Chapter 3.

2. Which of a rattlesnake's body parts did you find most interesting to read about? Why?

3. Which body part helps a rattlesnake sense heat from nearby animals?

    A. its rattle
    B. its tongue
    C. its pits

4. How does sensing heat help a rattlesnake hunt?

    A. The snake can find prey even in the dark.
    B. The snake can find warm dens in the snow.
    C. The snake can know where to hide.

5. What does **bask** mean in this book?

Like most reptiles, rattlesnakes are cold-blooded. They bask in the sun to stay warm.

    A. to lie in a warm place
    B. to go deep underground
    C. to stay somewhere cold

6. What does **skim** mean in this book?

Their bodies skim sideways over the sand. Only small sections touch the ground at a time.

    A. to dig a large hole
    B. to move quickly and lightly
    C. to stay in one place

Answer key on page 32.

GLOSSARY

cold-blooded

Having a body temperature that matches the temperature of the surrounding water or air.

deserts

Areas of land that have few plants and get very little rain.

digest

To break down food so the body can get energy from it.

habitats

The places where animals normally live.

hibernate

To rest or sleep through the winter.

prey

An animal that is hunted and eaten by another animal.

rodents

Small, furry animals with large front teeth, such as rats or mice.

venom

A poison made by an animal and used to bite or sting prey.

TO LEARN MORE

BOOKS

Humphrey, Natalie. *Diamondback Rattlesnake: North American Hunter*. New York: Enslow Publishing, 2022.

Perish, Patrick. *Sidewinders*. Minneapolis: Bellwether Media, 2019.

Rathburn, Betsy. *Diamondback Rattlesnakes*. Minneapolis: Bellwether Media, 2018.

ONLINE RESOURCES

Visit **www.apexeditions.com** to find links and resources related to this title.

ABOUT THE AUTHOR

Libby Wilson is a retired librarian. She loves to research and share amazing facts about nature with readers. She has met one rattlesnake in the wild. It just wanted to be left alone. She was fine with that.

INDEX

B
babies, 21
bite, 8–9

C
cold-blooded, 19

D
den, 4, 6, 19
digest, 26

F
fangs, 6, 9, 24

H
habitats, 12, 16
hunt, 8, 22, 24

M
mating, 21

P
pit vipers, 25
prey, 9, 24–26

R
reptiles, 19

S
scales, 12
sidewinder, 13

T
tail, 14

V
venom, 8–9, 24

ANSWER KEY:
1. Answers will vary; 2. Answers will vary; 3. C; 4. A; 5. A; 6. B